TIME FOR KIDS READERS

Clues
TO LONG AGO

by Elena Martin

Harcourt
SCHOOL PUBLISHERS

Orlando   Austin   New York   San Diego   Toronto   London

Visit *The Learning Site!*
www.harcourtschool.com

We can learn about a time long ago.

We can look at photographs and art made long ago.

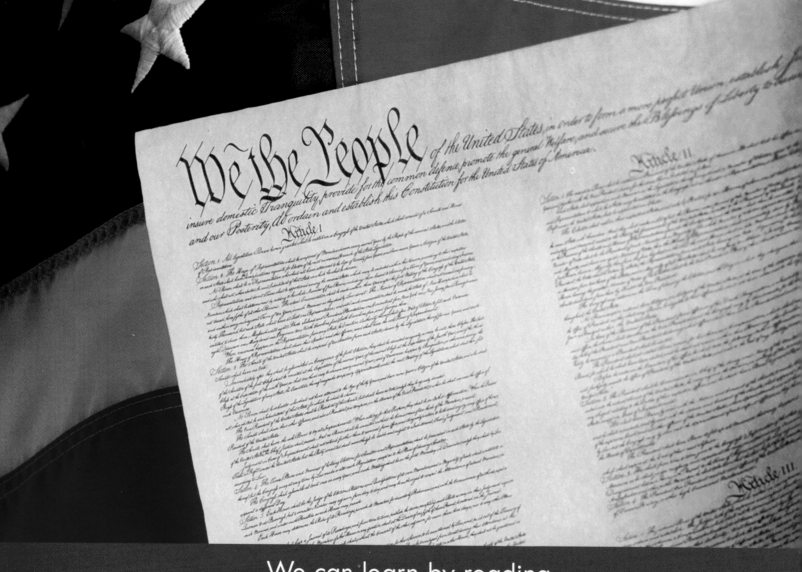

We can learn by reading

and by listening.

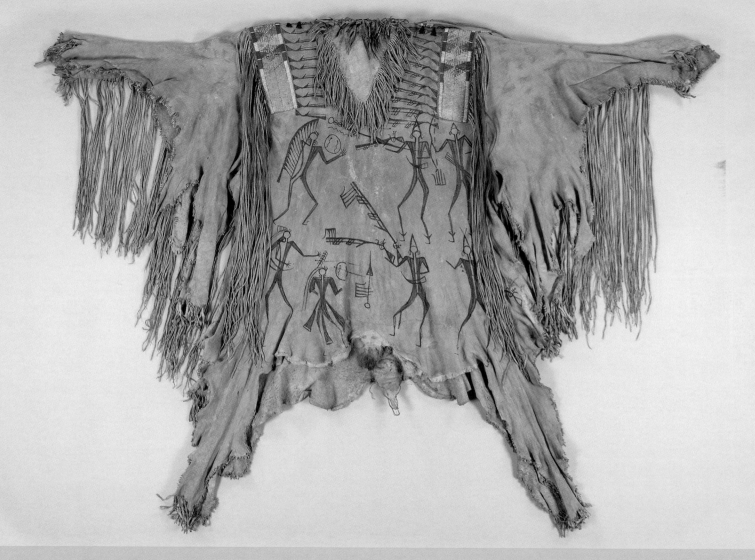

We can learn by looking at what people wore.

We can learn by looking at things used for work.

We also learn by looking at things used for play!